LAVA LAMP POEMS

LAVA LAMP POEMS

BY COLLEEN HIGGS

Publication © Hands-On Books 2011
Text © Colleen Higgs 2011
P O Box 385, Athlone, 7760, South Africa
modjaji.books@gmail.com
http://modjaji.book.co.za
ISBN 978-1-920397-25-8
Book design: Natascha Mostert
Cover artwork and lettering: Hannah Morris
Printed and bound by Mega Digital, Cape Town
Set in Palatino

Some of the poems have appeared in earlier versions in
the following publications: *Carapace, New Coin, Pumpkin
Seeds, Green Dragon, African Writing Online, Difficult to
Explain* and *Incwadi.*

Thank you to Colleen Crawford Cousins,
Finuala Dowling and Robert Berold for
editorial comments.

For Kate,
my burning brightly pilot light

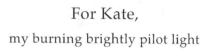

contents

notes from a new country

flying off the handle

I'm tethered very lightly, if at all
a horse who only thinks she's tied,
but every time she starts or gets a fright,
she finds in fact she is no longer near the handle   at all.

I'm easily startled, flustered, worried or disturbed
not manageable even to myself,
like a dog who is not quite tame,
I snarl, lose my patience,
sometimes I feel I could even slap strangers,
for no apparent reason.

swingball

Game. "Come inside now. It's dark."
After game. She wants to win one,
beat him, once. All day he won every game.
"Just one more game." The girl is trying.
"Persuade them to stop," their mother shouts.
Just on and on. The sound of ball hitting bat.
Thwack.   Thwack.   Thwack.

The grass begins to smell damp from the dew.
Relentlessly. It's getting dark. "You can't play swingball all day."
His head with the bat. He shrieks, the girl hits her brother
on the back of the head.
Their father says to her,
"Just you wait till we get back." Her sobs.
"Please don't hit her.
It wasn't her fault, Dad, it was mine."
The boy's head is covered in blood.

She waits and waits.
She is not punished. "I've got 12 stitches," her brother says proudly.
It's late on Christmas Day,
the two children.

the other side

She's making a dash for it, a skinny girl with dark plaits
her pale cotton dress tears on the stone wall, eyes alert to snakes
she's making a dash for freedom, for the other side
in the distance she hears her mother's voice, little bruises decorate her legs
she hides in the long kikuyu, climbs through snagged-tooth wire fences
she dreams of the mountain burning, she follows
her dreams – face red hot, feet on fire

From the car, she stares wistfully at carcasses, covered in flies and dust
skin, dried blood, only bone left now
the guidebook helps her work out which animal – the horns a vital clue
The riverbed stinks of mortality
the fine red sand gets up your nose, you can't pretend
it won't happen to you

Each day the lawn spits up bits of broken glass, concrete chips, twirled wire
and she is me/her mother/my mother and now
my daughter's long bones sculpt her firm smooth skin
my heart is squashed too tightly into my chest
Dreaming, hoping like hell my little girl won't fall out of the window
as I wallow in my shallow warm bath, cleaning, cleaning my feet

My first therapist, my first husband, my first father, my first lover, my last job
sticking all the bits together, painstakingly gluing each piece in the dark
All day drag my desires behind me, strands of hair snag in hours passing
my grandmother's faded blue nightie rides up her thighs,
her skin baggy from overuse. I steady myself at the kitchen counter,
pouring coffee, scalding into a cup
The day sets like jelly all around me.

my grandfather and other ancestors

As he got older my grandfather became more and more difficult. Refused to co-operate, gave everything way. What he didn't give he sold. I bought my grandmother's art deco dining room table and four chairs. Two were already gone. All the family silver, their furniture, his clothes. All gone. Except for a small, elderly suitcase filled with photographs and letters. Medals. His ceremonial sword.

After he died, I flew to East London with my mother on SA Airlink. She like a small, pettish dog, on a leash for the first time, straining to slip free, had to be managed. He'd been living in a residential hotel. The Quigney, before it was gentrified. Wide painted cement corridors, cooking smells. His room was large and light, two single beds, a TV, a fridge, a wardrobe. A small en-suite bathroom. His toothbrush, a glass, a squeezed tube of Colgate toothpaste.

We found him at the undertakers, already in a coffin. White shroud. Shrunken, his cheekbones high, still handsome. My mother brought him a suit, a white shirt, a tie, underpants. Socks and shoes. I imagined the undertakers would dress him in the shirt, tie and jacket. Leave him naked from the waist down. Why waste a good set of clothes? Why cremate a pair of nicely polished leather shoes?

"My girl" he would say to me. His Edinburgh accent. He held his head up high, chin up. Cheese. He loved cheddar and Stilton, sliced thinly. Good marmalade. Whisky. Rugby and cricket. And fishing. Old black and white photographs of him in the Transkei, late 40's and 50's holding up a huge fish he'd caught off the rocks. Some of the fish taller than him. Basutoland Mounted Police first and then later NRC – the 'native' recruiting agency for the mines.

My father's dad was born in Basutoland, lived near Zastron, buried in Mohaleshoek. My mother's grandmother ran a trading station at Thabo Bosigo. OBE for her good works with 'native' children.

My father drank too much, my mother slept too much and was prone to sulking. Depression. She had at least one affair, and smoked dope for a while. Tennis. Polo. I smacked my sister when she messed with my stuff. My parents paid our 'servants' slave wages. We were 'thrown out' of Lesotho, my parents' work permits refused.

I'm not nostalgic for the past, just aware of how short a human life is. I miss my grandpa. I miss being a child and eavesdropping on the grown ups while they sat on each other's stoeps. Drinking, gossiping, smoking. I miss Lesotho and our big gardens. All the rented houses we lived in. I miss my brothers and my sister and our nannies. I miss my parents. And their friends. Some of them are still alive.

1986

1986, my first year of teaching
kids on the Near East Rand
white kids who didn't love poetry
who hung out at Eastgate for a jol

1986, a year of being under surveillance, even if you weren't
a year of living in a flat called Homelands
a year of being disapproved of by my boyfriend's parents
the year his brother came out to them
the year his mother went to bed for two weeks

1986 was ten years later
it was deep in the dark bleak suffocating ages
of conscription, corporal punishment
swimming galas, rowdy staffroom jokes
netball coaching, too much marking

Now, the air is not so toxic
even though we still step
over (or around) the ruins

the comfort of parquet

I don't miss those years of pert
jacket swinging hopefully down two flights of stairs
into the car headlights, streetlights, warm bars, sexy strangers
nor the flirting and longing and prowling ahead

I don't miss the phonecalls, and the waiting and
arranging, and rearranging and driving, and analyzing
sifting, drifting, endlessness

I don't miss waking up in men's beds
men I hardly knew. Perhaps I miss
the way you could lean over and kiss someone
or touch him lightly on the thigh
Except, mostly I couldn't
do it like that, wasn't so cool, so nonchalant

Instead my mind raced, What will it
mean? Will he like it?
I couldn't just be a young woman sipping
whisky in the gloominess of a jazz club
leaning over to the man she happens to be sitting next to
and kissing him because she wants to

I miss the Market Theatre, Jamesons, Kippies, Rumours, Scandalos
the Black Sun, film festivals, installations, walks in wet November
streets late at night. But not the too finely tuned
anxiety of all that was going on around
and within me – crushing, brutal, oppressive –
and didn't seem about to end any time soon

All was taut, tense
Not sinuous, relaxed, sensual
except when waking alone and stumbling
from bed to bathroom in the sleepy coziness
of semi-wakened, semi-dreamwalking clarity
feet heavy on the parquet.

excuses

his father died when he was 11
when he was 28
his mother's a bitch
he's tired, he's overdoing it
his father beat his mother
he's insecure
he was adopted
he's stressed out
he's shy
he's had too much to drink
he drinks too much
he works too hard
he's very bright
he's not bright enough
his parents were fascists
his parents were communists
he's very sensitive
his parents got divorced when he was a kid
his father was violent
his mother was an alcoholic

my Yeoville

Where were you when you could play
freedom fighter, a dangerous game,
a particular way
of being worried about spies?
And who was really ANC and who wasn't.

And we danced. The Lurchers. The Yeoville Rapist.
Weird and wild and strange. Sex, drugs.
Because I lived there it was wonderful,
and the library, Tandoor, the Harbour, Midnight Express
Elaines, Rumours, Mamas.
The park at night, the path, the plane trees
the police station. Yeoville Checkers.

Bigger and wider and smaller my world was then
realised how much and how many
were mostly Zulu speakers
and so many who didn't speak any English. Only Serbian.
Any night of the week on Rockey Street
there wasn't one uniform
if you liked, you could fit in.
You could go and experience something–
come in from the cold
from Alberton, Kempton Park.

By the mid 90s the banks started redlining,
kickstarting slumlording.
You could hear buses changing gear
from the bedroom at Homelands.
One day the swimming pool opened to all.

from a balcony

for G

On New Years's Eve, a couple of years before the millennium
we stood on the balcony of your house in Troyeville
high in the dark sky, lights below
and distant fireworks, bangs like gunshots,
bursts of colour — shouting, hooting,
the air vibrating

We stood there, I'd made a decision
only later I'd feel the pain of.
That night on your balcony I was happy
the air was warm. I'd been to your hairdresser in Illovo
and paid more than I believed possible for a haircut

I felt sexy and courageous in my short hair
and my new life ahead. All of this was visible to me
as I stood there, free and full of possibility,
inviting the new to flow into the empty space I was clearing

I didn't see the pools of tears, the anguish
at leaving the stone house, the white stinkwood trees
which had grown tall and shady in the five years I knew them.
I didn't see the progressive rage
I would feel about a vacuum cleaner

I didn't see how I would go beyond all of that
to where I truly wouldn't care, wouldn't mind
about the vacuum cleaner,
or the books,
or the trees

It's not quite true that now I don't care, don't mind
in fact I am pleased that those things exist, that they are there,
and that they aren't mine.

From a balcony you can see far into the future
much is visible from a balcony

and there's so much that you can't ever see

unfinished things – a lament

on the table

a stone

curled up on

its haunches

like all my

unborn babies

the poet and the woodcutter

The husband invited the younger man into his home, to build more shelves. He was a poet, the older man. He had small hands, rather like bear paws in a children's book, and nearly as hairy. He could lie on his couch and visualize the new shelves. He couldn't build them, or not easily and effortlessly. So in his largesse, he gave the younger man a job.

The younger man was down on his luck, between things, staying with his sister. He was able-bodied, and had large, tanned, capable hands. He was dangerous because in spite of being down on his luck, he was tall, dark, handsome. He looked like a prince disguised as a woodcutter. He wore a black hat at a jaunty angle, he smoked cigarettes that he rolled up himself. Sometimes he drove by on his motorcycle on his way to swim at the dam. Sometimes when he rode by he wasn't wearing a shirt.

So, he came to make shelves for the poet. The poet's wife made him cups of tea and tried to think of things to talk to him about. He didn't chat much but he smiled easily, and made her laugh with the odd throwaway comment.

The poet's wife was also a writer. Of course she couldn't read her work to the poet; he was a real writer, a serious writer, a poet. He needed silence and he needed to listen to difficult jazz music. He needed to read the work of other serious poets who lived in Germany, Turkey, Israel and Poland – not the ramblings of his own wife.

The poet's wife took to reading her work to the woodcutter; let's call him that, the silent, tender-hearted woodcutter. He listened to her poems and stories and she could tell he found them moving from the way his eyes crinkled up softly as he listened.

The poet was often away on important business, giving readings, signing books, being interviewed, appearing on stages, meeting with other famous writers in big cities here and abroad.

The poet's wife was often alone in the big house with the new shelves and the tin roof that rustled in the wind. Or she would have been if not for the woodcutter who came round sometimes for a cup of tea, or to listen to her reading. Some days he walked past instead of riding the bike. He stopped and asked her to go with him to the dam for a swim. One particularly hot summer's evening she went swimming with the woodcutter and decided that she would go and live with him in the forest and become a real writer herself. And so she did.

cheap thrills

Porn magazines
my mother used to sell them
in the 70s at a bookstore in Maseru
Large sexy girls, big breasts thrusting
the arousing Letters page and the stories
stirring something I didn't know how to name.
In spite of early exposure, porn is
not something I developed a taste for,
perhaps because it was associated with my mother.

I allow myself short daydreams, brief fantasies
about people who don't belong to me,
men, usually, who are out of reach.
I've settled now, for this one particular person, my husband.

Yet it's not like before where I'd flirt and invite the person for a drink
lend them a book, call them for some spurious reason,
it's not like idly lighting a match
setting fire to a R20 note or the kitchen curtains

now I know for sure where these things lead

other women

I use Nivea, L'Oreal, sometimes Body Shop
I can't bring myself to spend hundreds of rands on what.
I like to see them arrayed on the dressing tables
and shelves of other women.

The bedroom is a little dark, a soft white duvet on the bed
cosmetics, perfumes, lotions, potions
a secret arsenal of sweet smelling beauty
tempt me in

If it's safe, I open a jar, scoop out a lick
onto my hand, smooth it in, feel the softness
seep into my cheek, like the loving touch
of mother, not mine, but the one in stories,
the one who wears an apron and has well groomed hair,
who knows what takes out red wine stains
who can diagnose chicken pox or yellow fever

In fact one of my mother's chief skills was diagnosing
and treating ailments. If she or the world had been different
she would have made an excellent GP
instead of being a woman who likes to visit doctors
for pills, potions, shots, ops, scans and tests.

I shut the jar, twist it closed.
Slink out of the other woman's room
and hope she won't notice that
I smell like her.

thoughts I started having about the Wimpy after I saw my ex-lover there with his long-lost-after-all-these-years American girlfriend

Wimpy Bars are one of those things you barely notice. You'd certainly never think of writing about them. They are background, white noise. They've been there as long as I can remember. As a kid it was a treat to have a chocolate milkshake in a Wimpy. Now they're in those Shell Ultra Cities on the N1 and other National Roads. They're clean and you always find the same ironed toast and just edible burgers and eggs fried in too much refined sunflower oil, the kind that comes in those 25 litre tins. They only serve instant coffee, but you can get rooibos tea. Sometimes in a Wimpy you'll hear a song you've forgotten about, haven't heard in over a decade.

Wimpys are there. Sometimes a Wimpy is your only option. You might even remember particular ones, if you travel on those roads more than once. I remember the Wimpy on the N2 outside Umtata, opposite UNITRA. I had a Hawaiian chicken burger, it came with a piece of pineapple. Pineapple means Hawaiian.

And then there's the one on the N2 closer to Cape Town, you have to go up some stairs to it. I've been there at night and in the day. Riversdale. I had a toasted bacon and egg when I was pregnant, by the time I got back to Cape Town I had to throw up. There are plenty of Wimpys I haven't been to. All those Wimpys in all those towns.

The Wimpy in Grahamstown was the only place in town open for a cup of coffee at 7:00 in the morning. It was the one he had breakfast at most Fridays. Why would you want to take a visitor from another country to a Wimpy? How does the Wimpy become a place saturated with meaning? The extra wors with the Sunrise breakfast – a vocabulary of intimacy? Why was I (if I'm ruthlessly honest) jealous?

You always remember too much of what doesn't matter to anyone but you.

on wanting a washing machine

She says yes, agreeing wholeheartedly, throwing herself into ideas like
camping for two weeks at Christmas with a toddler in the mountains near
Worcester. She says yes, but feels maybe, or perhaps, or no. The more she
thinks about it, the heat, how there is not enough shade, and how organized
she will have to be, the more she wants to say no. But she can't say no, like
others of her generation and background, yes falls too easily from her lips, or
OK as tepid as bathwater left overnight.

She remembers an earlier self, one who vowed never to have a washing
machine, or other appliances that were the trappings of late 20th century
capitalism. What could she have been thinking of, poor girl? Doing her
washing by hand, sitting for hours in a Laundromat, having her mother's
household take care of it? What? She didn't want to be tied down with stuff,
debts, repayments, instalments. She wanted somehow to be floating free of
all that.

stroke

My mother has had minor strokes. Brain infarctions.
Stroke: a word full of tenderness and aggression
and terrible consequences

I long for my mother
and I don't want to see too much of her.
I'm afraid she'll drag me down.
Drown me.

My mother is slowly forgetting her life
Who she is and what holds her together.
She forgets more each day
as though forgetting was a job. She will forget everything in time.

I try to remember harder, for both of us.
I hope I die before I forget my name, and how to drive
and who and what I love, and how to read, I want to
remember enough to follow the pebbles all the way
back into the dark forest.

fish

The day my father died, he marinated fish.
White fish steaks, thinly sliced onion rings, and lemon juice.

He died on the golf course.
He kissed my mother goodbye, she was napping.

When she woke up, he was dead.
Before he went to play golf, he marinated fish.

A week later, after his funeral, I threw the fish out.

missing horses

My father's hands were big and tanned
the backs covered in dark hair
he was a sportsman
good at polo, golf, squash, darts, tennis
a man with exceptional hand-eye co-ordination
and he could draw horses
from memory

In the second half of his life
he missed horses, every day,
horses were his inner life
he yearned for horses, to be among them
to ride them
to smell the hot sweat of horse after a polo match
to hold soft leather reins in his hands again

My father only once ever laid a hand on me
he wasn't given to hidings
he wasn't an affectionate man either, not to me
I loved him because I knew
how sad he was about the horses —
my mother made him choose
it's either me or the horses, she said

when someone dies

"It is those we live with and love and should know who elude us..." –
Norman Maclean *A river runs through it.*

After my father's death
I discovered it was too late
to try and get to the bottom of who he was
all the information I had, was all I was going to get.

When someone dies
they leave in their wake so much to do,
to sort out, papers, wills, documents,
bank accounts to close, a house to sell.

Parents are the most mysterious and most familiar of all.
My mother, her voice, her being, so familiar like the air I breathe
yet there is something about her that eludes me. She is
my oldest dream, the one who was there before
the beginning

make her breathe
keep her safe

I unbutton my heart as I cross the threshold of the Neonatal ICU,
into the place of waiting; the sacred high tech inner temple
where my baby lies in a glass cocoon.
Machines beep. Everyone pays attention.
For ten weeks I sit on the black moulded plastic chair next to her incubator,
waiting   for her to grow, to learn to suck.
The doctors, high priests in blue scrubs or chinos dispense opinion,
hope and medication. The nurses administer – amongst other things – love.
I'm one of the parents, humble supplicants, attending our babies
patiently as pilgrims. I hold her close to me in both hands
for hours each day. When I'm not with her my body aches
with loss and anticipation. My tiny alien creature alone, but not entirely:
she's attached to wires and tubes.

sleep deprivation

I sleep on a narrow ledge. Easily fall off.
My knees buckle, my back aches,
I blow sturdy bubbles that turn into dream children.

I forget to put my phone on silent,
I'm awake, staring at the red digits on the clock
coping by mice steps.

Plovers start up crying at the river.
The dog wants to come in, woof,
go out, woof, come in, woof.

It's all improvising,
My daughter sleeps attached to me like a limpet,
I can't think in a straight line.

marriage

The birds have all gone, the river is fuller
the days are shorter, and the rain is coming.
My life will end. I've seen it now, I've seen the face of death.

They came and wheeled your mother away
on a metal trolley. Instead of mohair or cashmere, they
covered your mother with a rough, grey blanket.

I can't know what you know, how you really feel
I can only surmise from how I see you spend your days
and what you come up with, what you have to show for it all after all

I'm here, not exactly waiting. I'm distracted,
busy, reading, preoccupied, thinking, dreaming.
But if you wanted to say something more to me
than paint colour, OSB, plywood, pergola, mast, tiller
screen, decking, boat, weather, wind, supper, diesel prices
I would listen.

Except, this is the way you talk to me of what is in your heart.
My own heart is thickened, hardened against your anguish.
There are gashes in our understandings
I can't know what you know.

(the last two lines come from a poem by Adrienne Rich)

swings and roundabouts

The jungle gym, the park, the swings
are the extent of your daily world for now.
You meet other children
other nannies, other mothers, while I'm at work.

Once as a student back packer in Barcelona,
I came upon a small park in a city block, buildings loomed
no grass, the ground tarred, the requisite slide, swings, roundabout, jungle gym.
small, bleak, foreign – yet familiar. Full of others' memories.

I will remember that you like the jungle gym the best
paint scarred, concrete pad below
climbing over the bottom bars, again and again
Or holding the bar above your head, your body slack.

Over and over you climb and hang
practising, building up your strength.
You play with such commitment
As though you're preparing.

Sometimes at night when you've crept into bed with me,
while you sleep you push against me with your strong legs,
its not kicking, its gentler and more precise
as if you're eager to push away. I'm your ground.

But first you're checking I'm there, before you step away
into your own unfurling life.

blaming Lulu

Kate loves to draw. 'I'm a drawer. You're a writer," she says. She draws
pictures of herself and of me and her father and the dog and her friends.
When she shows me the pictures I wait for her to tell me what she has
drawn, I don't always get it straight away. I rely on her to interpret for me,
to translate. "This is a plate of cupcakes. Here's a shark and a monster. This
is Barbie." She loves Barbie best, a golden haired goddess, fairy godmother,
princess, close friend, alter ego.

And then there's Lulu, her 45 year old inherited doll. Lulu is always the one
to blame, she drops and spills and breaks things, she is badly behaved and
angry and has mumps and no friends and is left to sleep outside or in the
garage as punishment. Poor Lulu, I'm always thinking. I identify with Lulu,
she's my old doll, her hair has been badly cut, she has koki scribbles on her
body and dirty marks on her face from countless plasters. She is the culprit,
the evil one, the bad, hard-hearted girl. She is feral and forgotten, deeply and
impossibly loved, even though she is scarred and unfortunate looking. Her
limbs and head can be pulled off and put back again.

she should be sleeping in her own bed

Most nights she still comes to our bed. One morning recently
it was after seven, and she still hadn't appeared.
I'll come when I'm ready, she said.
It's almost time to get up, I said.

Mostly I love having her in the bed with me, with us.
Even though she squeezes me to the edge
of the bed. Her body is warm, her limbs strong and vital.
Asleep she looks like an angel, long dark lashes on her smooth
cheeks. She smells hot like bread and warm grass.

"She should be sleeping in her own bed."
Somewhere in the world, there is an expert
who knows the truth of the matter.

At night she'll call to me, slightly panicky,
Mama… Does she know something about me that I don't know?
What I think is – she still misses me
she was in an incubator for 2 months as a newborn baby,
when she should still have been close to my heartbeat.

an ode to Perry

Perry Higgs
you're a soft dog, a salivating, patient dog
You're a Black River dog
a stench of rotting-mud-clinging-to-you dog

You're a blonde-fur dog,
a catch-billory-once-a-year, soft-eyed soppy dog
You're an expectant, happy sort of dog,
a blonde dog with wings and long waving tail

You're a sleep-through-intruders, curled-up-in-a-warm-
dreaming-ball dog
You're a wait-to-be-invited-onto-the-bed dog,
a scared-of-jumping-into-the-back-of-the-bakkie-for-a-walk dog

You're a dog who listens for my car and watches
for the sliding gate, a resolutely escaping dog
You're a bark-at-the-post-man dog,
a stand-and-take-your-punishment-by cold-water-hosing-down dog

You're a pedigreed dog, a highly recommended family dog,
a jump into the lei-water-canals-in-Nieu-Bethesda dog
You're a dig-holes-in-the-lawn-to-catch-moles dog,
a carry-shoes-and-socks-around dog

You're a dive-into-water, any-kind-of-water, fling-yourself-
into-the-sea-after-stones dog, a no-holds-barred kind of dog
You're a galloping-across-green-grass dog,
a disturbing-the-seagulls-in-the-river, sniffing

You're a sniffing, a following-your-nose-and-your-heart
kind of dog.

who are you?

Pippi or Annika?
I do my homework, worry and am a little timid
Pippi is strong and fearless, she makes social blunders
My daughter is Pippi, I have to be the cannibal king, even though in my heart
I know I am Annika. Annika brushes her teeth, is eager to please.
In the story, Pippi has no mother. Her father is the cannibal king.
"What do cannibal kings do when they aren't cooking people in large pots?"
"Reign. They reign, mommy."

wolf soup

In our version of *The Three Little Pigs*, we have them making
Wolf Soup at the end, but they remove the fur.
Who would want to eat soup with fur in it?

The third pig rescues the first two from the wolf's stomach,
they bath, and then they all live happily ever after.
Except no-one really does, it all comes to an end, sticky or not.

Either it will be bloody, furry, gory, or a fading away.
There might be vomiting, diarrhea. In the end, something will kill you
even if it isn't the big bad wolf.

when granny died

When your mother got her diagnosis, she said, *I just want six more years, three score and ten*. And I could tell she felt short-changed.

The day your mother was cremated, it was pouring with rain. You were wearing a jacket, a new tweed jacket. You drove to the Maitland Crematorium. You knew where to go. May 17th, a Wednesday. For other people it was a work morning. The chapel was functional. We were allowed half an hour in the chapel with the coffin and the body. An usher stood at the back. We didn't have a service. We just sat there quietly for half an hour. Your mother's friend made sure we received the correct ashes and not the ashes of someone else, such mix ups are not uncommon, she tells us. She went so far as to bribe an official.

Your mother died early on a Sunday morning, Mother's Day, you hardly slept. You knew she was dying, so you stayed with her. Kept a vigil.

I didn't want Kate to know we had cremated her granny. It seemed barbaric somehow to have burned her. I'd been fudging that one. I was okay for her to see her granny getting ill and terribly thin and vanishing and not speaking and for Kate to hold her hand and to sit on her bed and talk to her. I wish I could remember more of what she said. *Don't worry Granny you are very old.*

On a day when Perry was digging holes under the Rhus, still too lanky and thin, its roots not yet tapped into an underground water source, I was worrying that the tree might die. *Like Granny?* Kate asked. *Yes*

everything in our house

Kate thinks the lava lamp I bought her father for Christmas two years ago is hers. She thinks everything in our house is hers.

Last night her great aunt, Tessa, from London, slept in her room. Kate doesn't want Tessa in her room.
"She's not my friend," she says.
"Not yet," I say.
"She must go. When is she going Mama?"
"In a week or so."
"But it's my room."
"Yes it is. But please let her use it."
"Why can't she sleep in your room with you and Daddy?"
"That's a thought."
And so on, until she concedes, "She can sleep in my room but she mustn't look at my toys. She must look at the wall."
"OK, I will tell her," I say.

Kate loves the lava lamp. It takes a while for the yellow wax to heat up and float languidly to the top where it falls again in bubbles and loops.
Sometimes we sit on the couch and watch the lava lamp in the dark.
It's not like watching TV.
We're not watching it exactly, we talk in that slowed down, profound, goofball way.
Our eyes on the lava lamp.

notes from a new country

Jeppestown, 1994

We stand outside the Jeppe police station waiting to collect the ballot boxes and ballot papers. They have to be brought by armed police to the polling station. My friend, our voting station chief, signs for them.

It is 5.30 am on the 26th April 1994, the moon sets over the city, the Joburg skyline, the tall buildings. It hangs there heavy and yellow. The sky lightens behind us in the East. We drive into the lightening sky to work for the IEC for three days that will change the country forever.

A powerful thought enters my being: I want to live. I don't want to die, not just yet.

We drive off followed by the police. For once it is OK to be followed by the police.

We are working in the first democratic elections. On the first day we go to a Chinese old age home in Bertrams to allow the elderly Chinese people to vote. Some of these voters lie in bed. Everyone over 18 is eligible to vote.

We lived to see the day. For three days we take turns at different tasks. We work for twelve or more hours each day. We are tired, we are exhilarated.

"This is your national ballot paper. Take it, make your mark." I feel like a priestess at some ancient, vital ritual. I hand out the paper. Give it into the hand of each person who appears before me. I give the paper to students, to hostel dwellers, to teachers, to domestic workers, to people, ordinary people. I know a few of them.

"I am Lord Aston, most people call me Lord." I hear him tell someone. He is an IEC observer. He has come to see whether we South Africans can manage a free and fair election.

I examine people's hands, they hold them out to me and then put them under the infra red light so I can check they have not already voted. The voters are innocent and trusting about this, like children showing their hands to their teachers to show they are clean.

Forest Town, 2005

I wake up, it is after midnight. I hear a calling-out in despair, a keening sound, I think it is my godson crying. It's raining hard. Through the soft insistent sound of the rain, I hear wailing and sobbing. I am spending two nights in Joburg. My ten year old godson's mother died a week ago. She took her own life. I am upstairs and he's asleep downstairs in the TV room, where for now he is rooted. I listen harder through the rain and I realise it is the animals from the zoo. I can't tell which ones, perhaps peacocks, donkeys, or even monkeys. I'm tired and overwrought, my imagination amplifies what I hear, it sounds like all the loss, all the sadness and anguish in the world, slightly muted by the thrumming of the rain on the roof, on the skylight and in the trees outside. I go downstairs, wide awake, my mouth dry from drinking whisky earlier. I am afraid I won't be able to go back to sleep. Everyone in the house is asleep and I can hear them sleep, their steady breathing. I go into the kitchen and cut a slice from a cake that someone has brought and I pour a glass of milk and take it back upstairs. The animals are still taking it in turns to wail and sob, keeping up their night vigil of despair and longing.

The Mount Nelson Hotel, 2006

I've just been to the launch of "The Year of Women in South Africa" which also commemorates the 50th anniversary of the Women's March to the Union Buildings in 1956. I was invited ostensibly because I am a poet.

The launch was at the Mount Nelson at 5.30 am – so early because it was to be televised for Morning Live on SABC 2. I found myself sitting at a table of elderly black women who were all veterans of the march. I was the only white person at their table, and younger by thirty or more years. I escorted two of them downstairs to the marble and gilt toilets when they needed to go, Clorence Peters (85) and Tuli Makhalemele (78). At one point Clorence took out her ID book to show me that she was indeed born in 1920 and then so did Tuli. So I took mine out too, to show them that I was born in 1962. A younger woman at the table asked me if I wanted to see the women's passes. She wasn't joking.

We ate sliced pineapple, pawpaw, strawberries, kiwi fruit served on large platters. Croissants and sweet pastries in baskets were passed around. Finally we were each presented with a large white plate of scrambled eggs, smoked salmon and sausage.

Tuli told me she is poor and doesn't get paid to do what she does, which is to help disabled and elderly people access the grants they are entitled to. She looks as though she might be in her late 50s, except for her teeth. She was dressed in a fitted ANC suit which she made for herself in 1994. All the ladies wore fabulous hats or berets. I was sorry my cell phone wasn't fancy enough to take pictures.

All of this was filmed for live television. Pallo Jordan gave a speech in which he announced a youth poetry competition. Three Cape Town high school girls asked the Minister questions, which he answered with easy facility. The presenter was glamorous and confident; she kept returning us to Vuyo in the studio in Johannesburg for the weather or the sports or whatever.

Only in South Africa do you get to have breakfast with MPs as they stage a heartwarming (propaganda) occasion where old women who have lived in poverty get to eat scrambled eggs and croissants on national television.

Robben Island, 2006

Seagulls circle and cry overhead as the *Susan Kruger* ferry chugs off to Robben Island. I'm sitting next to Amron, an American volunteer librarian working at the Centre for the Book with me. Elizabeth Magakoa from Ekhurleni sits on the other side of me. The morning is overcast, the skies low and threatening. I wish I'd brought an umbrella and a woolly hat. Angifi sits across the way, framed by sea and moody skies in his technicolour dreamcoat styled from woven West African cloth. I don't know where Mandla is. I feel ever so slightly queasy, inhaling diesel engine fumes mixed with fresh sea air.

The *Susan Kruger* is one of the original prison ferries – today carrying mostly librarians, as well as old age pensioners from Elsie's River who heard about the special R20 trip to Robben Island with a free lunch thrown in. Little do any of us suspect that on the return trip we will be drenched and some throwing up the free lunch as the *Susan Kruger* lurches back to the harbour through heavy seas and driving rain.

The Robben Island Museum has invited three Community Publishing Project grantees and me as part of a panel of guest speakers for their 2006 World Book Day seminar, "Books that changed my life".

The pensioners aren't interested in the programme or the speakers. But the librarians are. The talks are inspiring, but it all goes on too long and then the weather changes. We eat lunch hurriedly before catching the bus back to the ferry. The cold rain batters down on us as we queue. We squash into the covered parts of the ferry – overcrowded, wet.

The trip back includes Island staff, school children, and us, the World Book Day people. Someone grabs hold of my coat, later there is a murky stain at the back. Vomit? "Keep your eyes on the horizon," someone else tells me. It sort of works.

Centurion, 2007

Last night I discovered that I've spent the last couple of days in Verwoedburg, which (wisely) has changed its name to Centurion. I am at an international multilingual/multicultural library conference. I am here because of the work I do in Community Publishing. Staying in a hotel in Centurion is like hanging out with someone in a witness protection programme.

The sky is blue and clear, winter is coming to an end here. Last night the Mayoral Function at Munitoria was even better than I expected. We were escorted on a long circuitous route through drafty corridors, greeted by a diorama of a Tswana village and library which delighted the foreign visitors, or perhaps amused them, whatever the case they were polite enough to appear delighted.

The Executive Mayor was suddenly unable to attend this function as something more urgent had arisen, even though the function was booked at least 6 months ago.

A minor dignitary was sent in her place. The minor dignitary and her companion were seated at a thatched podium far away from the conferees. We were treated to a number of choral musical items by students at TUT (Tshwane University of Technology). One of the numbers, "Mashini Wam", had the student singers miming shooting the guests with automatic weapons; this they performed in a low key, relatively unthreatening fashion while they danced. The musical items concluded with a newer, hipper version of "Sarie Marais".

Supper consisted of a small side plate onto which you could pile chicken thighs, crumbed deep fried chicken, fried fish balls, beef skewers, samoosas, white bread cheese sandwiches and a fruit skewer. We were each allocated one glass of pre-poured box wine or juice.

The speeches toed the party line and were padded with much friendly yet menacing goodwill.

Praise for *Halfborn Woman*

" The poems mine the most personal territory, and there is considerable tenderness and vulnerability. In poem after poem there is a steely clarity, naming pain and fragile love without flinching, allowing the dark dimensions of peopleís feelings to reveal themselves even while the hope and realisation of love is allowed to blossom. The consciousness of a mature artist is at work in all these poems. "

Karen Press

" Higgs's simplicity of language reads like pencil sketches -- a few strokes create a locally recognisable living form. "

Silke Heiss in *New Coin*

Colleen Higgs launched Modjaji Books, the first publishing house for southern African women writers, in 2007. Her first collection of poetry, *Halfborn Woman*, was published in 2004. She lives in Cape Town with her partner and her daughter.